Learn from Fossils

Contents | Page

written by John Lockyer

Red Rocket Readers™
Engineered by Flying Start Books

We can find fossils in some rocks, stones, and cliffs. We can dig them out. They are bits of ancient animals.

A dinosaur skeleton is a very old fossil. Plants can be fossils, too. Fossils can be hard to see.

A fossil begins when a plant or an animal's bones get stuck in mud. No air can get to them, so they cannot rot.

Then the mud and plant or bones turn into hard rock. It will take a long, long time.

A fossil can be all of the plant or animal. It can be just a part of them, too.

sea shell fossils

Fossils pop up in unexpected places. We can dig up shells on the top of hills. Now that is odd.

Fossils can get stuck in tree sap.
It might be an ant, a fly, or a bug.

We can dig up fossils near the sea. We might see them in rock pools or in the sand.

If we do see one, then you will need some tools. You can cut a fossil out of rock with a pick or a drill.

You can join bits of bones and
plants, so they look right.
This lets us see what bits are lost.

Many fossils are extinct plants and animals. They tell us what was on the planet a long, long time ago.

extinct

Dinosaur bones tell us how big it was. They tell us how it ran and how old it was.

Not all plants and bones turn into fossils we can see. Many fossils turn into gas and oil.

Cars, vans, and trucks run on this gas and oil. Fossils give us energy for our homes, too.

oil drills

Make a fossil.

You need: clay, a hard shape like a skeleton, paint, and a paint brush.

1. Roll the clay.
2. Press the shape in then pick it out.
3. Let the clay go hard.
4. Paint your fossil.